ROGUES & REBELS

Lawbreaking in the Forest Hundreds 1779–89

ROGUES & REBELS

Lawbreaking in the Forest Hundreds 1779–89

by Dorothy Paddon

First published in 2012 on behalf of the author by

Scotforth Books, Carnegie House,
Chatsworth Road, Lancaster LA1 4SL

ISBN 13: 978-1-904244-77-6

Printed in the UK by Short Run Press Ltd

Contents

Notes

Illustrations

Illustrations in text are by Thomas Rowlandson from the 'Dr Syntax' series of stories by William Coombes (1820). Though produced later than the decade covered in the article, the styles of dress shown are quite close to those in late 18th century prints by Rowlandson.

Digital images courtesy of Tony Nicholls, 'Past Pages' (www.pastpages.co.uk).

Other illustrations:

Waltham Abbey Gunpowder Mills: print supplied by 'Past Pages'.

The Villa of John Elsee Esq, Chigwell Row ; supplied by 'Past Pages'.

Chapman & André, part of *Map of Essex 1777*.

Family Names

Personal names have been kept throughout. They may be of interest to local family historians who, at this interval of time, surely need not be too embarrassed by revelations of ancestral misconduct, or too proud to find a forbear serving as a magistrate or parish office holder.

There is a database containing names of victims, accused, parish officials, witnesses, magistrates and judges – many more than are mentioned in this story. Unfortunately the database is in a very early, 'DOS' programme – itself a piece of 20th century history – which I could not transfer into a 21st century equivalent. However I am willing to search it for answers to queries.

Dorothy Paddon

Preface

THIS IS A SNAPSHOT of life in the South West corner of Essex during the decade before the French Revolution and the wars that followed, and before most ordinary men (and of course women) had the vote, and before many could read or write. Whilst births, marriages and deaths were recorded by the parishes, and communal events such as markets, festivals – or riots – were noted, individual accounts of people's lives, in diaries or letters, are harder to find. But when people came into contact with authority – parish, manor, magistrate or judge – then, in varying amounts of detail, records were often made of what they said, as claimants, employees, victims or witnesses.

The lower courts (Magistrates' courts and Quarter Sessions) dealt not only with serious crimes, which were referred to the higher courts (the Assizes, the Old Bailey), but also with petty crimes and with breaches of regulations, and many administrative matters nowadays handled by local authorities.

The words 'lawbreaking' and 'offence' have generally been used here in preference to 'crime'. Many of the offences recorded are clearly crimes, but a few are less serious breaches of the rules which, though covered by statute, would probably not be regarded as crimes by many people at the time, and by most of us now – swearing, owning a greyhound without license, allowing vagrants to sleep in your barn, or shouting at the Overseer of the Poor – offences surely not of 'Rogues', but perhaps of the 'Rebels' in the title.

This article began life as a long essay for the Open University MA in History. For that, we were required to focus on numbers. But statistics can be an uncertain business in history, especially in the history of crime. Figures may be less reliable or illuminating even than those we get from the Home Office today. The human stories interested me more, and so I noted them whilst researching, and can tell some of them here.

Dorothy Paddon

...We have erred, and strayed from thy ways like lost sheep.
We have followed too much the devices and desires of our own hearts.
We have offended against thy holy laws.
We have left undone those things which we ought to have done;
And we have done those things which we ought not to have done...

General Confession – Book of Common Prayer 1662

Rogues & Rebels: Lawbreaking in the Forest Hundreds 1779–89

IN THE LATE 18TH century the south-west corner of Essex had something of a bad reputation, with the highest incidence of property crime in the county.[1] What was it about the area and its people that led to this unwelcome distinction?

Some answers may be found in an early record of the Epping magistrates' bench,[2] an 'examination book' which recorded cases occurring in the ancient Hundreds of Ongar and Waltham between the years 1779–89. This gives us a brief glimpse of the crimes which contributed to this reputation, and more generally, a picture of the lives of people who lived in this district over 200 years ago.[3]

The judicial centre of the old Ongar Hundred was the market town of Epping, although it lay just over the boundary in the smaller, neighbouring Hundred of Waltham, which it also served. The two Hundreds had much in common; both adjoined Becontree Hundred in the south – which was later to be absorbed into London – and both comprised mainly small farming communities with, together, just three larger market towns. The Royal Forest of Waltham (now called Epping Forest) spanned the shared boundary, though the greater part lay within the Waltham Hundred.[4]

---

1 PJR King. *Crime, Law & Society in Essex 1740–1820*, unpublished PhD thesis, Cambridge, 1984. King has since published extensively on the history of crime.
2 Epping magistrates' Examination Book, Essex Record Office, p/em4.
3 Cases were followed up in rolls of Quarter Sessions (ERO – q/sp, q/sr), Assizes (Public Record Office, now National Archives, pro assi94) and in Minutes of the Forest Court of Attachments (EFO – rfw/ca).
4 Victoria County History – Essex, iv, v. Also Chapman & Andre, *Map of Essex* (part) 1777.

In 1974, the areas of these two ancient Hundreds, their borders only slightly changed, were brought together under the new Epping Forest District Council, after more than 100 years of fragmented administration.

Life in the two Hundreds

The population of the Hundreds grew quite rapidly during the last two decades of the 18th century. By the time of the first available Census (1801) it was around 18,000. Most people lived in the rural parishes, ranging from very small – Norton Mandeville with fewer than 100 souls – to large and expanding – Chigwell, with over 1,000.

The oldest town, Chipping Ongar, which in Saxon times gave its name to the Hundred, by late 18th century had been overtaken in population size by Epping with 1,812, and Waltham Holy Cross (which then included Waltham Abbey) with 3,040. Each of the three towns had a market and shops, and Waltham Cross, because of its position on the navigable River Lea, also boasted a number of mills, not only for grain, but for the manufacture of pins, silk, calico and gunpowder.[1]

Links with the City of London by coach or carrier were available two or three times a week from Ongar, Epping, Waltham Cross and points *en route*. These allowed gentry and City merchants to 'commute' between business and their country houses, and local tradesmen and farmers to supply markets in the capital with goods & produce. But for most people at that time life was still bounded by village or market town, where livelihood depended on the success of harvests and the goodwill of local worthies – gentry, clergy, merchants or professional men. Even before the deprivations caused by the wars with France, parish Poor Rates in the area increased considerably between 1776 and 1785, with numbers on out-relief or in the parish poor-house growing steadily during the decade.[2]

1 Victoria County History – Essex, iv, v
2 VCH E, iv, v.

Law & order in late 18th century

There was no formal police force at this time, although in London the Bow Street Runners, established earlier in the century, were precursors of the first professional force, the Metropolitan Police, formed in 1829. Rural parishes and small towns relied upon Constables recruited from the local community by the Manor Court (where surviving) or by the Vestry,[1] and sworn in before the local Justices. Constables were unpaid and undertook their duties in addition to their normal work.

Prosecution of crimes had to be undertaken by victims themselves, although in some areas property owners banded together in associations 'for the Protection of Property and Prosecution of Thieves'.

One such in Essex was "A General Association of the County against 'Murderers, Housebreakers, Highwaymen, Footpads, Stealers and Maimers of Horses, Oxen, Cows, Sheep and other Cattle" – a body which met in Chelmsford, advertised crimes discovered and offered rewards for the apprehension of perpetrators.[2] Poorer victims must often have decided against pursuing their case. Few of the accused or the victims were legally represented in the courts.

The 18th century is notorious for the harshness of sentencing – by the end of the century, under what was later known as 'the Bloody Code', almost 200 offences carried the death penalty – not only the gravest crimes of murder, or arson – but also forgery, stealing horses or sheep, destroying turnpike roads, stealing goods worth more than one shilling, being out at night with a blackened face, or (as an unmarried mother) concealing a still-born child. This list is not exhaustive. However, judges were sometimes unwilling to proceed to a capital sentence and as the century went on increasingly used their discretion to substitute a sentence of transportation,[3] service in the military or on the barges which dredged the Thames.

---

1   Vestries, or church councils, acquired an increasing number of civic functions from the times of Elizabeth I (and the first Poor Law) until they were replaced by separate civil parish councils in 1894.

2   See Chelmsford Chronicle July 1779 ERO

3   Transportation to America ceased in 1776 with that country's independence. Transportation to Australia began in 1787. In the intervening years prison ships (hulks), Thames dredger barges, and 'improved' gaols were brought into use.

A Court of Justice

Favourable character references from influential friends of those accused who were able to call upon them might bring about a reduced sentence, or even a royal pardon.

Altogether, this was a rather different system of policing and justice from that we have today.

In the Hundreds of Ongar and Waltham, the Royal Forest of Waltham (now Epping Forest) was an important part of the economy, especially in villages such as Loughton, which lay close by. The land, vegetation, and game of the Forest were the property of the Crown, but traditional rights and specific licenses to use or take these resources, in a controlled way, had been granted to members of forest communities over centuries. In addition to the general courts and system of law enforcement, the prosecution of offences against forest laws – unauthorised enclosures or the taking of timber or game – as well as the granting of licenses, were the responsibility of the 'Court of Attachments' for the Forest.

Lawbreaking in the villages

Loughton

In the first available census, in 1801, the population of Loughton is recorded as 681. During the decade 1779–89, 15 offences were recorded which involved either an accused person who lived in the village, or events occurring there. These were heard either at the Petty Sessions (Magistrates' court) in Epping or at the Quarter Sessions or Assizes at Chelmsford,[1] or before the Forest Court.

Joseph Webb, sometimes known as Joseph Parry, yeoman & ex-militia man, was prosecuted in March 1781, along with William Lynn of Epping, for entering wood-grounds in Loughton, and "cutting and carrying away several bodies of trees and other wood". The prosecutor was William Ford, the woodward for Miss Ann Whittaker of Loughton Hall in whose estate the woods lay. The case was heard at Epping before magistrate the Reverend Thomas Abdy Abdy. (The seat of the Abdy family was Albyns, at Stapleford Abbotts) Thomas Powell, bricklayer, a witness, reported seeing the two men unloading the timber at William Lynn's house in Epping. Webb (alias Parry) was fined 5/- for 'having in his custody wood and bodies of pollards 'for which he was unable to give any account'. He also paid 5/- costs of the court.

Blacksmiths and farriers in the village were vulnerable to thefts of iron. At the Summer Assizes in 1784, smith John Laybank made his case against William Mills, labourer, that Mills had taken from his smithy in Loughton "one iron plough coulter, a cellary and chain, and one iron gate thurible".[2] Mills was sentenced to a public whipping and 6 months in the House of Correction.

Since early in James I's reign, each county was required to provide a House of Correction, sometimes known as a Bridewell, after the first one in London. The Essex House was in Chelmsford, and there petty criminals and 'social' miscreants were put to hard labour for a term of months or at most two or three years, in an attempt to reform them.

---

1   Quarter Sessions (ERO q/sp, q/sr); Assizes (PRO assi94).
2   A thurible is a pierced incense burner, as used in churches (OED). Iron seems a rather unusual metal for this, and 'gate' is also puzzling.

5

A later and more serious case was the theft from Roger Enever's smithy in Loughton of 12 cwt of iron, with a value of £7/4/-. Carrying away over half a ton of iron could not have been unobtrusive, so may have been done at night. Charles Wilkes, labourer, of Loughton, was found guilty of this at the Lent Assizes in 1789 and sentenced to be transported to Australia for 7 years.

Also at the Lent Assizes of 1789 two charges were laid against another Loughton man. John Moore, a labourer, was charged with stealing a pig from farmer Robert Taylor and another from farmer George Bearfield. Moore was found guilty of both offences, and sentenced to a fine and 9 months in the House of Correction. Fortunately for Moore, the theft of a pig was not a capital offence, unlike the theft of a sheep or horse. Another pig-stealer, John Andrews, alias Mondham, had been found guilty two years before at the Assizes of the theft of 6 live pigs worth £3/5/- from John Arewater's farm in Loughton, but he was still 'at large' and no sentence was recorded.

Records show that enclosure of Forest land was not a pursuit of only wealthy and ambitious landowners. Two labourers, unnamed, of Mutton Row, York Hill, had enclosed a sizeable area of land and sown crops there. The Justice in Eyre[1] sitting at the Court of Attachments at the King's Head, Chigwell in 1789, ordered that the land be thrown open again, but only after the two men had 'got off their crops'.

Between 1779–1789, seventy presentments for breaches of Forest law were recorded, arising not just in Loughton but throughout the two Hundreds. Forty were for unauthorised enclosure of forest land, and 10 for lopping or taking trees. In addition there were 17 breaches of the game laws: 3 for hunting deer, 9 other game – mostly hares – and 5 for unlicensed possession of guns or game dogs.

In fact only 43 of the seventy cases were heard by the Court of Attachments in session at the King's Head, Chigwell. In 1770, a dispute between the Verderers of the Forest and the Warden, the Lord Tilney, over his nomination for Steward – one Sir Peregrine Bertie, a local worthy and magistrate of Walthamstow – dragged on for an astonishing 15 years, during which the business of the Court was largely abandoned. Thomas Hatherill, Keeper of the Loughton Walk, was concerned that many breaches of the game and

---

1 Justice in Eyre i.e. Chief Justice of the Forests

enclosure laws went un-prosecuted during this time. The Court began sitting again in 1785, and dealt with a backlog of cases, but in the meantime 18 cases had been dealt with summarily by the magistrates at Epping, and 9 referred to Quarter Sessions or Assizes.[1]

Chigwell

In 1801 the population of this parish, which then included Chigwell Row and the area now known as Buckhurst Hill, was recorded as 1,351.[2] In the recent decades the parish had seen rapid growth, particularly to the east of the Roding, which was a popular country location for successful merchants and professional men – the beginnings of a 'desirable' suburb. During the decade 1779–89, 29 offences originating in Chigwell were heard either at Petty Sessions or in the higher courts. By the early years of the next century Chigwell had a recognized 'crime problem' with 207 arrests within four years (1828–32)[3].

Although Chigwell's newer residents were prosperous and apparently law-abiding, the poor of the parish were a constant source of trouble. Christopher Hare, overseer of the poor in 1783, complained to the Bench that Suzanne Cracknell had two bastard children and refused to indemnify the Parish against the possible expense of supporting them. The father of the first, she had said at bastardy examination[4] in 1781, was 'Country John', whose real name she did not know, though 'he worked for farmer Richard Huddle last haytime'. The father of the second child, she said, was William Bales of Milk Street, Wapping.

Bearing an illegitimate child was not viewed as a crime, but as a potential claim upon the Poor Rate. The mother was required to name the father so that the cost of the child's upkeep could be recovered from him. But under an Act of James I reign, a woman who bore several illegitimate children and was

---

1 Minutes of the Court of Attachments, ero/rfw/ca. See also Richard Morris, *The Verderers and Courts of Waltham Forest in the County of Essex 1250–2000*, Loughton & District Historical Society, 2004, pp 80–1.
2 VCH Essex, iv.
3 VCH Essex, iv. .
4 Bastardy examination. Women having borne or being about to bear a child out of wedlock, who was likely to become a burden upon the parish, were obliged to appear before the magistrates to identify a father who could be charged with the child's upkeep

The Villa of John Elwes Esq.r Chigwell Row.

GENTLEMEN'S VILLA - CHIGWELL

unable or unwilling to identify a father could be prosecuted as a 'lewd woman' and punished by incarceration in a House of Correction for 12 months.[1]

John Sheering, overseer of the poor in Chigwell in 1787, complained to the magistrates that Elizabeth King, spinster, was a 'lewd woman' who had 'by her own confession three bastard children, two of which are chargeable to the parish'. He prayed that she be punished according to the Act'.

Though many poor victims of crime must have hesitated to bring a case before the magistrates, two unusually determined Chigwell women did come forward. In 1785 widow Sarah Hunt was gleaning – a traditional right of the poor – in the field of Farmer Edward Holroy (or Holroyd). Holroy told her to get off his field, but she insisted that she had the right, at which point he pulled out a stick from his coat and began to beat her on her back and shoulders. And then, as Mrs Hunt reported to magistrate Rev. William Gould, when her neighbour Sarah Troomans came to her aid, Holroy began to beat her too. Mrs Troomans stated that Holroy would 'murder her, against the peace'. Such conflicts over gleaning were on the rise, as 'improving' farmers, applying new methods to increase the yields from their acreage, began to reject the old country way of allowing gleaners, generally women and children, into the fields after harvest. Perhaps Farmer Holroy was a

---

1 This punishment was modified later in George III reign (1810).

member of the Harlow Mutton Club, which met to dine and hear lectures on agricultural improvements.[1]

But another 'old country way' – stealing livestock – was still pursued by a few. Several Chigwell men were accused of horse-stealing, which was a capital offence. In 1787 James Harris was accused with Thomas Chapman of taking a bay mare worth 50/- from Thomas Young – but found not guilty despite the evidence of three witnesses. In 1789 John Hicks was accused of taking a mare valued at £5 from the premises of Stephen Hunt; Hicks was found not guilty. Less fortunate was John Woollard, accused of the theft of a horse, with saddle & stirrups, from Robert Denham's stable; in 1787 he was sentenced to hang, and no record of remission of this sentence was found.

At the Lent Assizes in 1784 farmer Richard Fuller accused Peter Vousmene, labourer, of taking a ewe valued at 20/- from his pasture in Gravel Lane; Vousmene was found guilty, and would have hanged, but the sentence was remitted to one year on the Thames dredgers. Three years later Farmer Fuller was again at the Assizes, prosecuting William Purkis and William Fox in the dock. Purkis & Fox were accused of taking two lambs, worth 40/-, but were found not guilty & discharged.

The game laws were invoked in 1782 when Daniel Gunby, park-keeper to Sir Eliab Harvey of Rolls Park, prosecuted Chigwell yeoman, Samuel Sycomb, over the death of a fallow deer within the park. Gunby reported that a grey-hound and a spaniel were seen to set upon the deer. As a yeoman, Sycomb may have previously been granted a licence to keep game dogs, but he claimed that he was not within sight of them when the attack occurred. No record of the outcome of this case was found. It may have been settled out of court.

Not so fortunate was Chigwell labourer Jonathan Parker, tried at the Assizes in 1784 for the theft of game and several 'tame' ducks, all valued at 5/-, from Thomas Nicholson also of Chigwell. Although Parker was already detained in Newgate, and was reported to be very sick, he was sentenced to the Thames barges for two years.

Chigwell afforded opportunities for stealing valuable items from wealthy house-holds. Leather shoes, the property of Thomas Burford, clerk, were stolen by his

---

1 AKJ Brown, *Prosperity & Poverty; Rural Essex 1750–1815*, Chs.1,2. ERO, Chelmsford 1996.

ROBBED WHILE ASLEEP

servant Edward Smith, along with a quantity of silver items valued at £40. The case was referred to the Assizes in 1779, and heard before Judge Knapp.

At the Lent Assizes of 1786 a spinster woman, Mary Maloney, was accused of burglary. Maloney was said to have entered the house of Hugh Vallance at 3 a.m. and taken curtains, clothes, stockings and spoons. She was found not guilty of burglary, but guilty of theft, and sentenced to spend 6 months in the House of Correction. (Was this a deliberate softening of the verdict by judge and jury, perhaps to avoid a death sentence on a woman offender?).

A similar sentence was passed in 1789 on another woman, spinster Sarah Bradley, for the theft of silver buckles and clothing from John and Stephen Clements of Chigwell.

Chigwell also had its own forgers or 'coiners', David & Elizabeth Pugh and James Curtis. They were accused on the evidence of a copper halfpenny of having been involved in 'coining' since 1771, it was said. After an unexplained delay, the two men were sentenced at the Summer Assizes of 1782 to two years on the Thames barges. As counterfeiting was a capital offence, they must have considered themselves fortunate indeed. Perhaps evidence of the extent of their crime was unclear. Elizabeth Pugh was sentenced to the House of Correction for 1 year.

Other Villages in the two Hundreds

Fewer offences were recorded for the smaller parishes in the Hundreds during this decade, both as would be expected because they had smaller populations, but also as a ratio of incidents in each parish to the number of its residents. [1]

No offences were recorded during the decade in the parishes of Stanford Rivers, Abbess Roding, Stondon Massey, Greensted, or Little Laver. Fourteen parishes had fewer than six offences recorded over the decade, amounting to less than 1 incident per hundred of population in each community.

Of the remaining rural parishes a few were notable in having a higher ratio of recorded offences, closer to rates in Chigwell, Loughton, and the three market towns. In Chingford in the Waltham Hundred, and in Kelvedon, Moreton and Theydon Bois in the Ongar Hundred, there were a number of residents who must have been very well known to the local magistrates.

Even in the more law-abiding parishes thefts occurred of small quantities of foodstuffs – flour, butter, grain, or occasionally poultry – and thefts of linen, calico, small items of clothing, or timber. These were crimes most probably driven by poverty.

Paupers and vagrants did not always comply with the law or with the attempts of their 'betters' to control the Poor Rate and maintain order in the parish. In 1783 magistrates Abdy and Barwick heard that Elizabeth Poulton, pauper spinster of Theydon Bois, constantly refused to work as she was required to do. She had been "put out to various places" of work but never stayed, and had "quit her last position and returned to the village almost naked". She had also burnt the furnishings of the parish house provided for her. Unfortunately the record does not show the decision of the magistrates, or any clue about how this woman's behaviour was understood at the time.

In the workhouse at Lambourne, the master Thomas Mead reported to magistrate Rev. Abdy in 1786 that Mary Pavitt, wife of James Pavitt, pauper, "hath grossly misbehaved herself", refusing to work and abusing him and his wife.

---

1 The only available population figures, those from 1801 Census, probably overestimate the resident population of some parishes in the 1780s, but perhaps by not too great a margin.

PART OF THE ONGAR AND WALTHAM HUNDREDS, FROM CHAPMAN & ANDRE'S MAP OF 1777, SHOWING THE EXTENT OF OPEN LAND AND FOREST, AND OF TOWNS AND VILLAGES, AT THAT TIME. ALSO SHOWN ARE THE PRINCIPAL HOUSES OF GENTRY IN THE AREA, WITH THE NAMES OF THOSE WHO CONTRIBUTED TO THE COST OF THE MAP'S PRODUCTION.

Yeoman William Baker of Theydon Mount was accused of harbouring vagrants on his property. And in Lambourne, labourer Robert Young was accused, at Quarter Sessions in 1786, of 'lodging evil disposed persons in his dwelling house and outbuildings'. He was fined 6 pence.

At Quarter Sessions, in 1788, William Dyson of Nazeing was also fined 6 pence, for "refusing to maintain his family", who had turned to the parish for assistance.

There were several breaches of the game laws. In 1786 Philip Thoroughgood, coachman to a landowner in Stapleford Tawney, reported to magistrate Abdy that farmer John Crouchman had been seen "with a leash of greyhounds and another dog trailing up and down the fallow ground and, as I believe, looking for hares, as the labourer working in the field told him that one had been seen the day before". Crouchman received a summary conviction.

In the same year William Purkiss reported to magistrates Barwick and Jackson that William Maynard, labourer, of Theydon Bois "keeps a lurcher dog which he hath seen to have a hare in its mouth, and which he believes is kept for killing game". He asserts that "Maynard is not qualified by law to have and keep any dog for the purpose of killing game".

Also in 1786, Joseph Titmuss, a victualler, was prosecuted by Ben Turner, blacksmith, on behalf of a Nazeing landowner, for shooting a hare, though he was "not qualified to kill game". Titmuss admitted that the hare "weighed 8 lbs", and so incriminated himself.

In Chingford, a brawl in an ale house involved yeomen John Lee, Israel Higham, and Joseph Ward, with the victualler Thomas Johnson. All were found guilty of affray and sentenced to the House of Correction for 1 month, and then to stand surety for themselves for a period of 3 months.

A curious case in Chingford concerned George Carter who was prosecuted in 1786 for burying his late wife Mary in a linen shroud. The prosecutor was Joseph King, a carpenter, who may also have been the undertaker there. The magistrates fined Carter £5. The case was a breach of the Burial in Wool Acts (1667–8) which required that "No corpse of any person (except those who shall die of the plague) shall be buried in any shirt, shift, sheet or shroud or anything whatever made or mingled with flax, hemp, silk, hair, gold or silver or in any other stuff or thing, other than what is made of sheep's wool only".[1] Carter may have used a linen shroud because, like many, he could not afford a woollen one; the £5 fine must have been an additional hardship.

During the decade there were a few more serious crimes in the villages which may well have been remembered and spoken of for some years after.

The death of William Ovley in High Ongar was recorded at the summer Assizes in 1787; he died of injuries inflicted by 'James Doe' – or, as we would now say, by person or persons unknown. With the victim dead – and in the absence of formal police or detective agencies – it seems no-one could be found to investigate or prosecute his case?

Also in High Ongar, in 1789, Richard Allen and James Morley were sentenced at the Assizes to the House of Correction for 6 weeks for the theft of three female asses – valued at 20 shillings each – which were the property of Joseph Woolmore and of John Bootle. (One of the witnesses at this trial bore the wonderfully 'Shakespearean' name of Charles Sipsack.)

In 1788–9 the village of Magdalen Laver was shaken by a scandal, when John Smith accused two labourers, Edward Speed and Richard Pool, of forging the will of the late Henry Cole Esq. in order to defraud him, Smith. An 'army' of seven witnesses attended[2] – it is not clear whether for prosecution or for defence – but the case was quashed. This controversy must have kept the village gossips busy for some time.

Further scandal surrounded a Navestock yeoman, Ralph Oakden, who stood accused at the Quarter Sessions in October 1789 of attempting to rape three men of the village. A record of the outcome in two of the cases was not found, but for the third Oakden pleaded guilty only to assault, for which he was fined ten guineas – a considerable sum.

Whilst the majority of those accused in the Hundreds at this time were from the lower or middling ranks of society, members of the gentry were

---

1 The Burial in Wool Acts 1667 and 1678 were passed in the reign of Charles II, when the wool trade was in serious decline. An affidavit was sworn at each burial stating that the law had been complied with. A penalty of £5 was imposed if wool was not used. The act was eventually repealed in 1814 but it appears to have been disregarded often before then.

2 These were Benjamin Smith, William Beamain, James White, William Mead, Thomas Wall, J Warner, James Montague.

occasionally brought before the courts. One such was Sir Edward Hughes of Lambourne. He stood accused by a Forest Keeper before the Court of Attachments in Chigwell in 1787, of taking large quantities of turf, loam and gravel from the Forest. It is not clear whether Sir Edward was himself punished for this, but the Court later issued a handbill warning against the taking of loam, gravel and turf from the Forest; this may show that up to that date such offences by landowners had been overlooked, possibly during the 15 years when the Forest court failed to sit.[1] Two years before, Sir John Conyers II, of Copped Hall, himself a magistrate, had also appeared before the Court of Attachments in connection with enclosure of Forest land for covert – cover for game. He agreed to open up the land.

Of three men from the villages accused of horse-stealing during this decade, two were sentenced to hang – Aaron East of High Laver, and George Spradbury of Theydon Bois. However James Reed of Chingford, who appeared at the same Assizes as Spradbury in Summer 1783, had his sentence transmuted to 4 years on the Thames barges. We do not know what influenced the judge in Reed's case to pass a lesser sentence. A transmuted sentence was also passed in 1784 on James Flack of High Ongar who stole 1 wether sheep, value 10/-, the property of farmer Edward Edwards; instead of hanging he was sentenced to serve 2 years on the barges. Charles Gibbs of Moreton was also found guilty of sheepstealing at Lent Assizes 1783, but record of his sentence was not found.

Lawbreaking in the market towns

Chipping Ongar

By far the smallest of the three market towns in the Forest Hundreds was the ancient market town of Chipping Ongar, with just fewer than 600 inhabitants (1801), one third those of Epping, and smaller even than several of the village parishes. Offences recorded in this town parish were few during the decade – only seven cases were noted.

---

1 Sir Edward Hughes is mentioned in the Victoria County History as living just over the parish bounds, in Chigwell, and as being one of several gentry who were noted benefactors of Lambourne parish at that time.

One concerned the local baker, Thomas Eaton, who was indicted at Quarter Sessions in 1779 for using false weights and balances in his shop. Perhaps more seriously, there were three significant thefts, two of which led to sentences of transportation. Two labourers in 1781, Thomas Houchin and John Thorogood, were accused by Thomas Allsop, and found guilty of the theft of £5 in monies – a sum warranting the severest penalty, though sentence was not recorded. James Vale, also a labourer, was accused by William Finch, at the Summer Assizes of 1784, of the theft from his dwellinghouse of many lengths of calico and other materials; witnesses included Elizabeth Finch, wife of William, John Linsley and Richard Guy (who had appeared also as witness against Houchin & Thorogood three years earlier – perhaps he was the parish constable at this time). Vale was sentenced to 7 years transportation, and so escaped the death penalty. Also to be transported for 7 years (from 1786) was labourer John Stevens who stole from John Pettit's workshop three clocks, four pairs of shoe buckles, a watch-chain – all goods awaiting sale or repair – and some pliers.

Epping

With a population approaching 1,812 (census of 1801) and 47 indictments recorded during the decade, Epping topped the list for reported offences as a ratio of population, among the village and town parishes of the two Hundreds. It may be that, as the Bench sat mainly in Epping, it was particularly easy for the townsfolk to bring cases before the magistrates.

By the last decades of the 18th century, Epping was a busy market town and coaching stop, with a flourishing market specialising in pork and dairy produce[1] and, as recorded in 1800, as many as 26 inns.

Some historians have suggested that crimes of violence diminished over time as people moved into towns and adopted 'civic' manners.[2] But in late 18th century Epping this transformation was still in the future; busy market days and the numerous inns gave many opportunities for heated confrontation.

---

1 VCH Essex (v) records a 'butter-cross', demolished around this time – hence present-day Buttercross Lane.
2 Howard Zehr, *Crime and the Development of Modern Society: Patterns of Criminality in Nineteenth Century Germany & France*, London: Croom Helm, 1976

A COFFEE HOUSE QUARREL

Bricklayer John Notley, with Charles Carey, breeches-maker, and Robert Butcher, servingman, were accused by William Garish and Samual Freeman of assault and battery and were served with recognizances of £10, and for Butcher, £20, to attend Quarter Sessions in 1779.

Failing to live up to his name, Makepeace Turner, gardener, was charged at Quarter Sessions in 1784 with assault on John Maudsley. This case was 'removed *a certiorari* to the King's Bench' – this may mean that Turner claimed he had not received (or could not receive) a fair trial in Chelmsford.

No sentence was recorded for Andrew Aley, labourer, of Epping who was accused of assault on Elizabeth, wife of Luke Newby, in 1788.

William Welch, parish constable for Epping during the decade, had a difficult job. James Hoare, labourer, confessed to assaulting Welch in 1788 – but surprisingly, was discharged. Not so Richard Stace, yeoman, who had refused to come to Welch's aid during this incident; he was fined 6 pence.

Sentence for a case of rape was not recorded. Samuel Cricks was found guilty at Summer Assizes in 1781 of raping widow Sarah Cole. There were several witnesses at the trial – Sarah Blows, Suzanna Blows, William Blows,

Alice and Christopher Sipsack[1] – though whether supporting the prosecution or the defendant records do not show.

In 1780 Samuel Mears, collarmaker, and James Haslam, shopkeeper (and collarmaker), were bound over for £10 each to keep the peace. Had there been perhaps a disagreement over terms of trade or employment?

It is not surprising that many of the incidents arising in this busy market town involved trade matters. In 1780 William Curtis, innkeeper at the Crown Inn, was prosecuted by Nathaniel Ashurst, a private soldier of the 2nd Regiment of Foot, for refusing to "receive and victual" him; magistrates Conyers, Abdy and Beadon fined Curtis £5. He seems to have been a controversial character – for in the same year he appeared at Quarter Sessions accused of selling ale without proper license – and was fined 40 shillings with 10 shillings costs.

Three years later, a William Curtis was accused under the game laws by Joshua Green, servant of local farmer Griffin, of hunting with a greyhound, catching & killing a hare on the farmer's land. The record refers to Curtis as 'the younger' so he may have been a relative rather than the innkeeper himself.[2]

John Haddon, Excise Officer, gave evidence before Magistrates Abdy & Barwick sitting at the Cock Inn, Waltham Cross in May 1785. "On 29 March last, I went to the house of yeoman Thomas Pinsent in Epping, and heard John Glasscock call for brandy & water, which was brought & paid for. I then called for two glasses of rum, which were handed to me. But I believe that Thomas Pinsent has no license to sell spirituous liquor." Another Excise Officer, Thomas Bloomfield was also at the house on 29 March, and appeared as a witness. Pinsent was convicted, but the penalty "mitigated to £5, to include expenses".

At the same session in May 1785, Thomas Fardell, yeoman of Theydon Garnon, told how he bought 39 pounds of pork – at £6 a stone – from Joseph Dorrington at his shop in Epping, having seen it weighed on the steelyard there. But only one hour later he had the pork weighed on his neighbour Thomas Webb's steelyard, and found it wanting a full 2 pounds.

---

1 A Christopher Sipsack appeared as witness 8 years later in the case of theft of three asses in High Ongar.

2 At a time when extended families often chose baptismal names from a small range, this may have been so.

He returned to Epping, when an argument with Dorrington ensued, but the shopkeeper refused to admit to selling short measure and would not make any allowance. The outcome of this case was not recorded.

Ann Draper, widow, was indicted in 1784 for using false balances in the sale of flour, and Joseph Lilly, chandler, two years later, for a similar offence; he was fined 5 guineas.

With the volume of goods being bought & sold and much traffic into and out of the town, theft and indeed robbery were not uncommon. Sometimes those accused were women, and the items stolen typical of women's domestic realm – foodstuffs, garments and cloth.

At the Lent Assizes in 1780, Jane Barnes was accused by Charles Freshwater of stealing cloth, a cloak and two bottles of cordial. She was found guilty and sentenced by Justice Knapp to 9 months in the House of Correction. Witnesses at the trial were Freshwater, Mark Jordan, & Joseph Dorrington – most probably the same Dorrington the pork butcher accused by Thomas Fardell some years later of selling short measure. Jane Barnes's name appears in the Chelmsford Chronicle at this time, as being charged at the Assizes with the theft of packages, from the London to King's Lynn stage coach at Epping, these being the property of Mr Lloyd of Swaffham and of Dr Smith of Fakenham, of value in total £1/10/-. These may be additional crimes, or possibly a slightly different account of the same crimes, noted above as recorded in the Rolls.

Jane Brown was accused by Jeremiah Crump, victualler, at Quarter Sessions in Chelmsford in April 1780, of the theft of a piece of pork. She was sentenced to imprisonment for three months. At the Lent Assizes a year later, Ruth Hogg, wife of Henry Hogg, labourer, and Alice, wife of Daniel Richardson, were jointly accused by Pearson Till, shopkeeper of Epping, of the theft of 13 yards of lawn worth £3. The three witnesses were Richard Brookes, John Freshwater and Thomas Champnoys. Record of the outcome of this trial was not found.

Judges in the higher courts in Essex, as elsewhere in the country at this time, would often hold back from imposing the capital sentence which was available to them under the 'Bloody Code' in cases of robbery and grand larceny (the theft of items worth more than one shilling). Nevertheless four Epping men found guilty of highway robbery during this decade were sentenced to

hang, and no record of remission was found. John Wells & John Sparrow were found guilty at the Lent Assizes in 1786 of robbing Edward Edwards of £10 in money, and were sentenced to hang.

Six years previously, brothers John & William Fenn, had been found guilty of robbing Isaac Aaron, a jeweller from Houndsditch, of a watch, chain, stockings, handkerchief, clasp-knife, and £3/10 in money, on the highway near Epping. They too were sentenced to hang.

Waltham Holy Cross and Abbey

Of the three market towns in the hundreds, Waltham Holy Cross (which included the area now known as Waltham Abbey) was the most industrialised. There had been mills on the River Lea there since medieval times, and in the 18th century and early 19th century these included a fulling mill, a pin factory, a silk mill and silk & calico printing works, breweries, and of course the gunpowder mills, which had been in production over more than a century.[1] During this decade the gunpowder mills, until then in private ownership, were bought by the Board of Ordnance (1787), and a period of expansion began.

---

1 VCH Essex, v, p164

POWDER MILLS, WALTHAM ABBEY.
_ Published by J. Ganford 122 Holborn Hill. March 24. 1804.

GUNPOWDER MILLS AT WLTHAM CROSS

Hence, Waltham Holy Cross was the most busy and populous parish in the two Hundreds, with resident numbers approaching 3,040 (census of 1801). Records were found of 61 offences involving inhabitants of the town parish during the decade, the highest total found among all the parishes.[1] However, this represented a slightly lower rate per head of the population than for Epping and even for Theydon Bois, Chigwell & Loughton. In fairness to the Waltham population in general, a large number of the recorded offences seem to have been committed by a small group of determined 'career' criminals, whose several trials took up much of the time at the Assizes in Summer 1785.

Thomas Littler, Thomas Abrahams and John Rumball stood accused by John Topham of burglary on his premises, during which a silver watch, and brass key, worth 40/-, and coins, were taken. Thomas Needham Esq accused the same men of breaking in & entering his house in the town, stealing feather beds, a looking glass and a coffee mill – goods in all of the value of £4 10s. 6d. Robert Denton, draper, accused Abrahams, Littler, Rumball, and another man, Samuel Hanson, of stealing a quantity of printed linens valued at £30.

Perhaps these prosperous victims had decided jointly to bring their prosecutions to the Assizes at the same time.

---

1 Note VCH Essex, v, p169 on concerns about increasing crime in Waltham, in early 19 century– as also for Chigwell.

22

A Thomas Abrahams, with others, was accused by John Pain of stealing a wether sheep worth 30/-. (If this was the same Abrahams, then clearly he was not a 'specialist' thief.) Abrahams was also found guilty at this Assize of the theft of 8 bushels of oats and two sacks, all valued at 22/-. Jonas Hampton was accused of receiving one of these sacks of oats, knowing it to have been stolen by Abrahams; he was found guilty, but was discharged.

There were even more indictments. Several men were accused of being involved at various times in thefts of large quantities of saltpetre from the gunpowder mills owned at that time by James 'Boucher' Walton. Chief among them were Thomas Abrahams and Thomas Littler, but also some lesser players – Samuel Bateman, William Kenyon and William Edwards – and once again Jonas Hampton, clearly unwise in his choice of associates. One incident involved the theft of 500lbs of saltpetre (value £50), another 300lbs (value £12) and a further 112lbs. How did these men plan to dispose of such industrial quantities of saltpetre?

'Lucky' Jonas Hampton was found not guilty and again discharged. No record of verdict or sentence for Bateman, Kenyon or Edwards was found, but Abrahams and Littler were found guilty of these, and of the several other crimes and were sentenced to hang. So also was John Rumball; although apparently not involved in the saltpetre thefts, his participation in the other burglaries & thefts was confirmed. But he went on the run, and a warrant for his arrest was still outstanding a year later.

These cases suggest that the development of industry in Waltham Holy Cross in the late 18th century was paralleled by the growth of more organised crime with a gang, apparently involving some leading and some fringe members, regularly stealing items for resale in the hope of making a good living in that way.

Other serious crimes in Waltham Holy Cross were prosecuted during the decade. A highway robber, John Moore, alias Pearce, was sentenced to hang in 1789. Earlier in the decade three men, Dawson, Brookes and Kay were also sentenced to hang for the same crime, but had sentence transmuted to service in the East India Company. In 1785 Lewis Williams was found guilty of stealing 100lbs of mill brasses from Walton's gunpowder works, and was sentenced to transportation for 7 years. Thomas Markwell was prosecuted for breaking & entering and the theft of clothing valued at 25/- from Arthur Heron's house; he escaped hanging but was sentenced to 14 years transportation in 1787.

Without more background information about trials and those accused it is difficult to understand variations in sentencing – the practice of judicial 'discretion'. What influenced judges at the Assizes in opting for a sentence of 'service in the East India Company', or on the Thames dredgers, rather than of hanging? Was it a man's previous record, intervention by persons of influence during the trial or after, or the workforce needs of enterprises in which 'good character' was of less importance than muscle? Similarly it is not always clear to the modern eye why one offence should lead to a sentence of 7 years, and another to 14 years transportation.[1]

Waltham Cross also had its 'lighter people',[2] those without serious criminal intent but willing to bend the rules now & then. Blacksmith Stephen Errington grazed horses on a common pathway. Philip Dawkins, victualler, kept a disorderly house, and was fined £10; John Randall was accused with him, but was discharged. And farmer Arthur Reed was fined for 'cursing and swearing'. He apologised to the magistrates in 1786 for uttering 'twenty profane cusses', in the hearing of Charles Alvery. He insisted that this would not have happened if he had not been drunk and, disowning his drunken self, he refused to pay the fine required. So this eighteenth century 'Sir Toby Belch' was committed to answer for non-payment at the next Quarter Sessions.

Overview

Has this brief tour of lawbreaking in the Forest Hundreds shed light on the observation with which it began – that "the South West corner of Essex had the highest incidence of recorded property crime in the county"?[3]

The information gathered was by no means complete. In particular, we did not look at records of the Becontree hundred which, lying south of the Ongar and Waltham hundreds and so closer to London, would have added significantly to the total of recorded crime in the South West of the county. But within the Ongar and Waltham hundreds we found a wide variety of recorded offences (not all of them property crimes) which reflected a growing diversity of the area's communities and local economies towards the end of the 18th century (see Appendix I).

---

1 See Douglas Hay: *Property, Authority and the Criminal Law* in 'Albion's Fatal Tree: Crime and Society in Eighteenth Century England', Middx, Alan Lane, 1975.
2 Wm Shakespeare, *Twelfth Night* – act V, sc 1 (Malvolio).
3 PJR King (op cit – footnote 1)

Most of the smaller villages had low levels of recorded crime, perhaps because offenders were not always pursued or prosecuted, and perhaps – as sociologists would suggest – because these small, close communities had informal ways of influencing conduct which were more effective than the use of courts and legal sanctions. With the exception of thefts of livestock (some of which were capital offences) village crimes were mainly thefts of small amounts of food, grain, poultry, cloth, or timber – opportunistic crimes possibly driven by poverty.

Looking at the amounts of Poor Rate levied in each of the parishes (and setting this against the population size of the parish) there was an inverse relationship between the level of Poor Rate and the number of recorded offences – for example, of the 7 parishes with the highest rate of offending, five had the lowest level of Poor Rate,[1] whereas for the large group of parishes with low or nil offending, the Poor Rates (where information is available) were at a higher level. A simple conclusion might be that generous 'welfare provision' (in its 18th century form) reduced temptations for the inhabitants to break the law. But without a clearer picture of how decisions about raising and spending the Poor Rate were made in the Vestries, we should perhaps reserve judgement (see Appendix II).

Breaches of Forest laws were, not surprisingly, more common in the villages close to the forest, such as Loughton and Theydon Bois, and so contributed to the higher incidence of lawbreaking there.

Chigwell parish – that part west of the river, now Buckhurst Hill – was also on the forest edge. But in addition to scope for breaking forest law, the recent settlement in the parish of 'new gentry' grown rich in London brought temptation to the unscrupulous in the shape of luxury items which could be stolen and resold at a good price.

Increased trade and movement in the area brought more occasions for crime. Forest roads, long notorious for highway robbery, were busier than before with coaches, carriers and individual travellers engaged in business between Essex and the capital. Thirteen men were accused of highway robbery during the decade; five were found not guilty, six were hanged, and two had sentence commuted to service with the East India Company.

---

1 Poor Rates – at mid-decade – VCH Essex iv,v.

The expanding towns of Epping and Waltham Holy Cross had the highest numbers of recorded offences in the two hundreds. With trade flourishing in the Epping market, the town's constable and its magistrates were kept busy throughout the decade. And in Waltham Cross the increase in manufactures enlarged its population and increased opportunities for the organised theft of industrial materials and products.

And a question to close: The following decade saw the beginning of the long wars with revolutionary and republican France. How many men from the two Hundreds were enlisted in the army? And was their absence, temportatily at least, linked to a lull in lawbreaking in these towns and villages?[1]

---

1 Clive Emsley, *Crime & Society in England 1750–1900*, 2nd edition, 1996, Longman Group UK, Ch 2.

Primary Sources

Epping magistrates' Examination Book: Essex Record Office (p/em4).

Rolls of Essex Quarter Sessions: Essex Record Office (q/sp, q/sr) and Assizes: Public Record Office, now National Archives; (pro assi94).

Minutes of the Forest Court of Attachments: Essex Record Office (rfw/ca).

Chelmsford Chronicle 1779–1790: Essex Record Office (microfiche)

Bibliography

Clive Emsley, *Crime and Society in England 1750–1900*, Longman Group UK, 2nd ed. 1996.

Douglas Hay: *Property, Authority and the Criminal Law* in 'Albion's Fatal Tree: Crime and Society in Eighteenth Century England', Middx, Alan Lane, 1975

PJR King. *Crime, Law & Society in Essex 1740–1820*, unpublished PhD thesis, Cambridge, 1984.

Richard Morris, *The Verderers and Courts of Waltham Forest in the County of Essex 1250–2000*, Loughton & District Historical Society, 2004, pp 80–1.

Victoria History of the Counties of England – A History of Essex, Vols iv, v. University of London, OUP, 1966

Howard Zehr, *Crime and the Development of Modern Society: Patterns of Criminality in Nineteenth Century Germany & France*, London: Croom Helm, 1976

Appendices

I Number & type of offences and court where verdict or sentence passed.

II Number of offences from each town and village parish, and level of Poor Rate.

Appendix I

Type of Offence at Court where verdict and/or sentence passed.

All records examined – 1779-1789:

Offence	Petty sessions	Forest Court of Attachments	Quarter Sessions	Assizes	Totals
No/little detail			34	11	45
Violence – not involving property	3		27	2	32
Taking livestock			2	20	22
Taking other property			6	77	83
False dealing	1		4	9	14
Trade	5		14		19
Forest laws	18	43	8	1	70
Social order	8		8		16
Total by court	35	43	103	120	301

Appendix II

Estimated rates of offending in each parish during decade 1779–1789.

Highest rates of offending

Parish	Nos Offences during decade	Population 1801	Offences per 100 pop.	Ratio of Poor Rate / population (mid-decade)
Waltham Cross	62	3,040	2.0	.3
Epping	47	1,812	2.6	.3
Kelvedon	9	360	2.5	.3
Moreton	9	360	2.5	.3
Theydon Bois	8	334	2.4	.5
Loughton	15	681	2.2	.6
Chigwell	29	1,351	2.1	.3

Medium rates of offending

Parish	Nos Offences during decade	Population 1801	Offences per 100 pop.	Ratio of Poor Rate /population (mid-decade)
Chingford	10	612	1.6	.4
Theydon Mount	3	196	1.5	na*
High Ongar	10	741	1.3	.6
Chipping Ongar	7	595	1.2	.4
Norton Mandeville	1	93	1.1	.4

* na = not available for this date

† Poor rates at mid decade = VCH E iv,v

Lowest rates of offending

Parish	Nos Offences during decade	Population 1801	Offences per 100 pop.	Ratio of Poor Rate /population (mid-decade)
Theydon Garnon	5	517	.9	.6
Bobbingworth	2	216	.9	.9
Magdalen Laver	2	228	.8	na*
Lambourne	4	515	.7	na
Navestock	4	623	.6	.6
Beauchamp Roding	1	169	.6	.6
Shelley	1	169	.6	.5
Leaden Roding	1	159	.6	na
North Weald	3	620	.5	.5
Nazeing	3	658	.4	na **
Fyfield	2	511	.3	.5
High Laver	1	346	.3	.4
Stapleford Abbots	1	320	.3	na
Stapleford Tawney	1	196	.3	na

* na = not available for this date.

** But note "squire's schemes to help poor help themselves" - VCH E, v, pp147-

No recorded offences

Parish	Nos Offences during decade	Population 1801	Offences per 100 pop.	Ratio of Poor Rate /population (mid-decade)
Stanford Rivers	0	740	-	.6
Abbess Roding	0	205	-	.7
Stondon Massey	0	200	-	.6
Greensted	0	102	-	.2
Little Laver	0	90	-	.8